Toads and Tessellations
A Math Adventure

Sharon Morrisette

Illustrated by Philomena O'Neill

ini Charlesbridge

2

It was not the easiest thing in the world,

being the son of a great magician. Enzo tried to learn magic, really he did. But his rain spell left pasta dripping from the village trees, and his Oro-e-ricchezze spell left Signore Baldiatto with flowing golden hair instead of a wealth of gold. Even his pot-of-plenty overflowed with soap instead of soup, although the entire village agreed it was very good soap.

"Keep studying," Enzo's father said. "And someday you will be a great *mago*, like me."

"I don't see how," Enzo replied, as he picked enormous slugs from his garden. He'd meant to grow giant melons, not mollusks.

"You just need to find your *own* kind of magic," his father said.

Enzo studied magic books, as his papa asked. But in secret he read others, as well: books by great astronomers, mathematicians, and physicists. "Oh, to someday be a *grande matematico,* like Galileo Galilei or Johannes Kepler," he dreamed, as he watched the stars wheel through the sky.

Then one day his studies were interrupted by a knock on the door.
On the doorstep stood Aida, the shoemaker's little sister.

"*Buon giorno,*" she greeted Enzo. "Is your father home?"

"No. He's away at a *mago* convention for the week," Enzo replied.

"Can I help you?"

6

Aida wrinkled her forehead. "It's my brother, Tessel. He has a customer with a rather unusual request," she said, and then hesitated. "She wants *twelve* pairs of shoes made out of *one* piece of leather."

"Who is this customer?" Enzo asked.

The door slammed open, and Bedhilda, the castle housekeeper, stormed into the room. "There you are, girl," she bellowed. "Have you found the Great Mago?"

Enzo sighed. So Bedhilda was the new customer. She hated spending money; but her charges, the twelve princesses, danced away their shoes every night.

"Uhh . . . he's away," Aida said. "But Enzo can help us."

"What?" roared Bedhilda. "This is no ordinary leather to be handled by a mere apprentice!"

"If you don't want my help, perhaps you should buy more leather," Enzo suggested.

"Insolent pup," Bedhilda hissed. "With or without your help, all twelve princesses must have a pair, or I will not pay! And I'll be checking your progress, too." With that she sailed irritably out the door.

"I see Tessel's problem," said Enzo.

"I thought you might use a stretching spell to make the leather bigger," Aida suggested hopefully.

"I don't know, Aida. I don't have a talent for spell casting," Enzo said.

"Please," Aida begged. "We need your help."

"I can try," Enzo agreed reluctantly. He fetched a spell book and followed Aida out the door.

They found Tessel in his workroom, staring at the piece of leather.

"What will I do?" Tessel cried. "She'll feed me to her cats—"

"She doesn't keep cats," Aida said, rolling her eyes.

"Or make me eat a turtle," Tessel grumbled. "I heard she made a blacksmith eat a turtle for not fixing a pot fast enough."

"It was only a snail, Tessel," Aida said, and then she motioned to Enzo. "The Great Mago's son is here to help us. He's almost a magician."

11

Almost a magician. The words hurt Enzo. Still, he looked at the spell book, took a deep breath, shut his eyes, and chanted:

"Expand, expand, expand, and grow,
A foot at least . . ."

Enzo faltered and looked at the book again.

". . . a giant toad."

There was a pop and a faint smell of smoke. Enzo opened his eyes.
Where once there was a shoemaker, now there was a pile of empty clothes.

Ribbit!

A stout brown toad stared out from inside Tessel's shoe.

"This is ribbit-culous," said Tessel the toad.

"What happened?" Aida asked.

"I think I combined two spells," Enzo moaned, looking back
at the book.

"Perhaps we should try a different spell," said Aida.

"No more experimenting with spells!" cried Tessel.

Something clicked in Enzo's mind. Signore Galileo's book talked
about experiments using math. Perhaps magic was not the only way
to solve this problem.

"Let's try a different kind of experiment," Enzo said. "A math experiment. Maybe that will show us how to use every scrap of leather without wasting an inch."

"That won't work," Tessel said. "The pieces of a shoe don't fit together perfectly. There are always leftover scraps."

"Perhaps . . . do you mind if I use this?" Enzo asked, as he gently dumped Tessel from the shoe.

"*Mama mia!* You're ruining my shoe!" Tessel exclaimed, as Enzo ripped it into pieces.

"Sorry, Tessel. It's for the experiment." Enzo laid the ripped pieces on top of the leather. "Drat! There are too many odd curves."

"What if we simplify the shapes?" said Aida. She trimmed the shoe pieces into rectangles and triangles.

"I see!" Enzo exclaimed. "By flipping and turning pieces, we can form a perfect perigon."

"No more magic! I don't want to be a perigon!" croaked Tessel.

"A perigon is a 360-degree angle," Aida explained to her brother.

"I guess it's a *kind* of magic," Enzo said. "We can flip, turn, or rotate pieces any way we want in order to *completely* fill a point. The internal angles of all the shapes at that point add up to 360 degrees and form a perigon, or round angle."

"Look!" cried Aida. "The pieces make a hexagon. We could repeat that shape across the leather like floor tiles, and we wouldn't waste an inch."

"Yes, but can we make twelve pairs of shoes using only *this* piece of leather?" Enzo asked.

"Oh, *si,*" said Tessel, nudging pieces into place with a flick of his tongue, "They'll be pointy, though, with all those triangles."

"No points!" Bedhilda shrieked, popping like a cork through the open door. Enzo rolled his eyes. She'd come to check on them, after all.

"Would you have people mistake the princesses for jesters?" she roared. "I want shoes for toes like these." Whipping off a shoe, she thrust out toes as fat as the slugs in Enzo's garden.

"No, Tessel!" Aida shrieked. But it was too late. Tessel's toady tongue darted for the tempting, grublike toes.

"Argh," yelled Bedhilda, hopping on one foot.

Without thinking, Enzo shut his eyes and chanted:

"Toady skin needs an antidote;
Take the form of a . . ."

Enzo faltered. What was that spell again? Oh, yes!

" . . . of a billy goat!"

Pop!

"You turned Tessel into a *goat*?" Aida asked in disbelief.

"It's not easy memorizing all these spells, you know," Enzo said.

"Incompetent fools!" Bedhilda laughed. "You have three hours to make my shoes, or I'll have you walking with beetles in your boots!" With that, she stormed out the door.

"This is baaaad," said Tessel the goat.

Frantically Enzo paged through the magic book, looking for something to break the spell. Then he heard a rip.

"This is goooooood," said Tessel, gnawing on a piece of his shoe.

"Drop it," Aida ordered. Tessel let the piece fall to the floor.

Enzo picked it up. It was only a nibble from one of the rectangles. He put it back, and then he realized it was on the wrong side. It was as if he'd taken the bitten chunk and slid it into a new spot, creating a curve that was large enough for a set of squirming, sluglike toes.

piece of leather

goat bite!

slide to other side

"Maybe there's more than one way to do this," Enzo said. "I can slide the nibbled piece to the other side of the rectangle without rotating or flipping it."

"I see," said Aida. "So we can repeat the shape with the curved side of one piece nesting into the indentation of the next. The pattern could go on forever."

"Exactly! No gap or overlap—a new form in a snap!" Enzo said, snapping his fingers.

Pop!

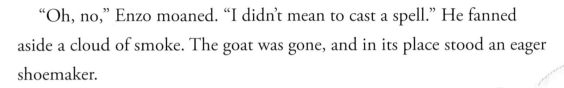

"Oh, no," Enzo moaned. "I didn't mean to cast a spell." He fanned aside a cloud of smoke. The goat was gone, and in its place stood an eager shoemaker.

"How did you do that?" Aida asked.

"Never mind that!" cried Tessel. "Quick, Aida! We have shoes to make!"

Three hours later, Bedhilda stormed through the door. When she saw twelve pairs of slippers lined up on the workbench, she scowled.

But after she tried on a pair and wiggled her toes, something unusual happened. A smile spread across her face.

"*Grazie!* These are perfect," she cried, scooping up the slippers.

"And my pay?" asked Tessel.

"Here, shoemaker," Bedhilda said. Then she waltzed out the door.

"*Che bello,* she paid me!" Tessel said. "Plus, we've invented a new way to make shoes. It's a revelation!"

"You could say it's a *tessellation,*" Enzo said with a grin.

"Of course!" Tessel said, slapping Enzo on the back. "I will be *famoso.*"

"Enzo, you are truly a great magician," Aida said, giving him a hug.

"Me? A great magician?" Enzo replied, surprised. "But I solved the problem with a math experiment."

"Then," Aida said with a smile, "I guess we'll have to call you a *grande matematico,* instead."

And suddenly Enzo realized that his father was right; he *had* found his own kind of magic. Knowing how to solve a math problem was all the magic he really needed.

GLOSSARY

flip: A flip occurs when a shape is moved to face in the opposite direction. This is also called a reflection, because the flipped shape appears as a mirror image of its original position.

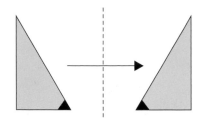

perigon: A 360° angle, or revolution. Also called a round angle.

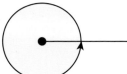

slide: A slide occurs when a shape is moved in one direction, from one place to another, without rotation. This is also called a translation.

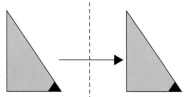

tessellation (tiling): A pattern of shapes that covers a surface with no overlaps or gaps.

transformation: A change in a shape's position. There are three basic transformations: flip, slide, and turn.

turn: A turn occurs when a shape is rotated in place. It's also called a rotation because the shape moves around a point like the hands on a clock.

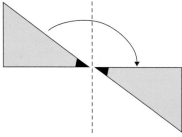

Did you find the tessellations?

There are at least twenty-six tessellations hidden in the pages of this book. Can you find them all?

Answer key: p. 1: floor under Tessel the toad; pp. 2–3: herringbone pattern on Signore Baldiatto's doublet, roof tiles, young girl's dress, windowpanes, and woman's kirtle; pp. 6–7: floor tiles and windowpanes; p. 8: Bedhilda's ruff; p. 11: bricks in fireplace, floor tiles, and windowpane; pp. 14–15: floor tiles; pp. 20–21: Bedhilda's kirtle, Bedhilda's ruff, floor tiles, and windowpane; p. 24: shoe pattern; p. 25: floor tiles and windowpane; p. 27: Bedhilda's kirtle, Bedhilda's ruff, and windowpane; pp. 28–29: brick wall, hem of tablecloth, and windowpanes

MATH NOTES

What is a tessellation?

A tessellation is a way to tile a surface with shapes so that there are no overlaps or gaps. Tessellations occur everywhere. You'll see them in floor tiles, soccer balls, honeycombs, and turtle shells. They can be very beautiful and complex—like those in ancient buildings or those found in the work of the famous artist M. C. Escher— or they can be as simple as the tiling on a bathroom floor.

Are tessellations really named after a shoemaker?

No, but isn't it a fun idea? Tessellation comes from the Latin word *tessella,* which means a small cube or a tile.

Can you really use tessellations to make shoes?

Yes, though there are probably better ways to make shoes. You can, however, use tessellations any time you want to use every bit of a material without waste. Tessellations are used in factories to cut expensive metal and in homes to make quilts, both in cutting the cloth and in creating the beautiful patterns.

What about Galileo and Kepler? Were they real?

Absolutely, and they definitely would have been Enzo's heroes. Galileo Galilei (1564–1642) was an Italian physicist, mathematician, astronomer, philosopher, and musician. He has been called the father of modern science. Johannes Kepler (1571–1630) was a German mathematician and astronomer. His mathematical works include the first systematic treatment of tessellations. Kepler was a key figure in the seventeenth-century scientific revolution.

Galileo Galilei

Johannes Kepler

To Abby, Alex, and Sophia. You always inspire me.—S. M.
Thank you Nick and Sue for all your support.—P. O.

Italian words
buon giorno: good day
che bello: how nice
famoso: famous
grande: great
grazie: thank you
mago: magician
mama mia: oh, dear
matematico: mathematician
si: yes
signore: sir

Text copyright © 2012 by Sharon Morrisette
Illustrations copyright © 2012 by Philomena O'Neill
All rights reserved, including the right of reproduction in whole or in part in any form.
Charlesbridge and colophon are registered trademarks of Charlesbridge Publishing, Inc.

Published by Charlesbridge
85 Main Street
Watertown, MA 02472
(617) 926-0329
www.charlesbridge.com

Library of Congress Cataloging-in-Publication Data
Morrisette, S. (Sharon)
    Toads and tessellations : a math adventure / S. Morrisette ; illustrated by Philomena O'Neill.
        p. cm.
    Summary: Even for an apprentice magician Enzo is not very good—but when
Tessel the shoemaker needs to use a single piece of leather to make twelve sets
of shoes, Enzo finds that when magic fails, math may solve the problem.
    ISBN 978-1-58089-354-1 (reinforced for library use)
    ISBN 978-1-58089-355-8 (softcover)
1. Magic—Juvenile fiction. 2. Magicians—Juvenile fiction.
3. Apprentices—Juvenile fiction. 4. Shoemakers—Juvenile fiction.
5. Tessellations (Mathematics)—Juvenile fiction. [1. Magic—Fiction.
2. Magicians—Fiction. 3. Apprentices—Fiction. 4. Shoemakers—Fiction.
5. Mathematics—Fiction.] I. O'Neill, Philomena, ill. II. Title.
PZ7.M829235To 2012
813.6—dc23   2011025785

Printed in China
(hc) 10 9 8 7 6 5 4 3 2 1
(sc) 10 9 8 7 6 5 4 3 2 1

Illustrations done using Windsor and Newton watercolors on Fabriano SP paper
Display type and text type set in Madrid and Adobe Garamond Pro
Color separations by KHL Chroma Graphics, Singapore
Printed and bound February 2012 by Jade Productions in Heyuan,
    Guangdong, China
Production supervision by Brian G. Walker
Designed by Martha MacLeod Sikkema